BUSINESS ADVISER'S CONSULTING & COACHING

Lothar E. Soliwon

Coeditors Christian Aguirre and Donaji Montes

CONTENTS

WHAT DO BUSINESS CONSULTANTS AND COACHES DO?..1
Consultants May Use Other Consultants 4
Overlap & Differences Between Business Consultants & Coaches ... 4
New World Order of Business 5
Avoid Layoffs 6
Major Technological & Societal Changes 6
Disruption of Consulting Industry 7

HOW BUSINESS CONSULTANTS & COACHES CAN HELP YOUR ORGANIZATION 8
consultants May Save You A Great Deal In The Long Run 8
Solve Problems 9
Tune Up an Organization 9
Validate Ideas 10
Advice on Technology, Investments, Marketing & Other Specialized Needs 10
Solving Marketing, Distribution & Sales Problems Globally 10
Software Consulting 11
Cybersecurity 12
Wellness & Fitness 13
Accurate Translation, Transcription and Interpretation 13
Corporate Governance Consulting 13
Television Programming Consulting 14
Interim Management 14
A Test Drive 15
Validate & Improve Ideas That Have Already Been Generated 15
Accountants May Help Improve Your Business 15
Attorneys Are Often Key Players 16
Project Management 17

Executive Business Coaching... 17
Training Staff.. 18
Marketing/Public Relations/Communications/Design/Media.......... 18
Medical Consulting 20
Political Consulting 20
Provide Fresh, Objective Views, Strategies & Plans 20
Assist With a Merger, Acquisition or Startup 21
Revive or Shake Up and Organization 22
Turn-key Projects 22
Managed Services.. 23
Scapegoat.. 24
Determining If Outsourcing Is Valid.. 24
Remote Experts Can Be Less Expensive... 25
Foreign Nationals Can Be Integral To Project Success................... 25
Complex Job Could Be Broken Up Into Several Consulting Jobs... 26
Buying & Selling Businesses 27

HOW DO YOU FIND THE RIGHT CONSULTANTS AND COACHES? 28
Consulting & Coaching Assistance on the Cheap 28
A Smart Friend 28
College Project 29
Internships 29
Score.. 29
Small Business Development Centers... 30

HIRING A PAID CONSULTANT OR COACH.................................31
Consulting Firms Offering One-stop Shopping for Expertise.......... 34
Involvement With Consultant... 35
Contracts & Compensation.. 35
ZG Worldwide Consultants Connects Clients to Broad Range of Human Capital.. 35

ABOUT THE AUTHOR 38
ABOUT THE COEDITORS 39

WHAT DO BUSINESS CONSULTANTS AND COACHES DO?

Since you have taken the time to get this book you are likely curious about what business coaches and consultants do. Maybe you need to broaden your understanding in this area since your business has problems that need to be addressed but feel you need to bring in outside assistance. This book approaches the subject broadly as to what business consultants and coaches do. Some readers may think it addresses services that are not truly business consulting and coaching. The providers of many specialized services consider themselves business consultants because they deal primarily with business, answer many questions and advise clients on how to make the best use of their services. They might also be called subject matter experts since they have a deep understanding of a topic, process or skill.

Consultants and coaches could well provide worthwhile benefits to your company, such as improve the use of technology or resolve its human relation problems. You may need help in figuring out how to be a better manager and could use someone to resolve issues within the company or with customers. You may think your business is stagnating and can be improved, have a gut feeling something is wrong but can't quite put a finger on it, or have specific needs for which you require experts. You may know people who hired consultants or business coaches and heard how helpful they were;

possibly you were told they were a waste of time and money. In many cases, these people may be right. Some experts may not really have the expertise needed. They may be going through the motions to look like they know what they are doing but actually don't have the skills they say they do. Other consultants may have been much more prepared to find better solutions.

Business consultants and coaches offer a wide variety of services for businesses, government agencies and nonprofit organizations. This condensed book provides a general, broad overview of these professions and gives insight about hiring a consultant or coach. After reading it you know much more about business consulting and coaching than the average business person. You will be able to use this information to improve your organization and help it achieve a higher return on its investments.

Coaches and consultants have been around a long time, serving small to large organizations. In the Middle Ages and earlier, kings and religious groups had their internal and external advisors. Military and political advisors as well as educators and clergy have also been very important for years for leaders in many organizations. Lawyers have long played a prominent role as personal and business advisers.

In the early 1900s business and management consulting started to grow and be more accepted as the business environment and technology became more complicated. Executives need help with strategy development, making their operations more efficient, better marketing, overall performance, improvement and integration of rapid advances in technology.

Since the 1960s business coaching and consulting have grown rapidly as more organizations recognized they needed outside assistance in dealing with many complex problems. Even the major multinational corporations hire consultants for supplemental assistance as they seek assistance in preparing for the future and solving problems as they arise. It is impractical to hire full-time people if they are only needed intermittently. New people have new approaches and ideas.

In simple terms, consultants and coaches are people who provide expertise and professional advice for a fee in many areas of business, personal life, health, employment, etc. This can vary from problem solvers who may spend months with complex projects or someone brought in for a short duration to meet a special need. The terms business and management consultants as well as coaches are often used interchangeably and are subject to individual interpretation. Some see business consultants as providing assistance with specific services such as accounting, information technology, finance and marketing, while management consultants delve deeply into the organization and skew towards improving overall business operations. Others see business consultants as helping smaller companies solve problems and make improvements whereas management consultants more broadly analyze how their clients operate and assist their management in making improvements. Some business coaches have very broad backgrounds that enable them to also offer in-depth management consulting services.

Because many specialized business services are very important to the operation and growth of a company, a consultant providing the service often does much more than come in and do the service. They may make recommendations on how to better integrate what they do into the firm's operations and make fuller use of the knowledge and expertise they provided.

Their plans and alternative strategies based on analyses offer guidance to organizations in preparing for the future. Larger organizations often have their own internal consultants who are used to solve problems throughout the organization, but even those with internal staff may use external assistance if the problems are complex.

CONSULTANTS MAY USE OTHER CONSULTANTS

Consulting firms, even large ones, often draw on consultants from other firms if they don't have the special expertise internally for a project. It's easier for the big consultancies to form multidisciplinary project teams since they usually have a broad network of expertise. Many consulting firms offer various degrees of international consulting. Modern telecommunications allows many types of work to be done remotely and has made outsourcing of expertise a huge industry. Many business consulting and coaching firms provide services internationally and cater to the needs and challenges of multinational organizations.

Many consultants give advice and alternative strategies for solving problems and may not implement their suggestions. Some companies want consultants who take this a step further by implementing what was suggested to them since they don't have the skills.

OVERLAP & DIFFERENCES BETWEEN BUSINESS CONSULTANTS & COACHES

Executive or business coaches typically are management consultants who improve the general performance of senior and middle management, but they also may work with the rank and file. They may be experts in a highly specialized niche for which the company needs answers. Some might say having a coach is a sign of weakness, while others think it improves the organization and is an adjunct to its human resources staff. Toxic work environment, lack of employee engagement and succession planning are among the reasons organizations hire business coaches and management consultants.

The functions of business coaches and business consultants have many other overlaps depending on the task at hand. The way this book is written is with much overlap of consulting and coaching in the narrative. A simplistic view of the differences is coaches have an internal organizational focus while consultants look outward at relations with other organizations and external variables. Coaches help improve the individual and act as a guide. Consultants make recommendations and solve problems. Some coaches also work well with helping a client to understand and think through dealing with issues in the external environment. What adds to the complexity is consultants, along with dealing with the external environment, may be faced with things going on with the individual that needs to be addressed that could be affecting how the firm interacts with extremal matters.

Coaches also may have an overlap with what psychologists do, and some are in fact trained psychologists. Life coaches would have more of a slant to psychology than a business coach. Some business coaches have significant business experience and education. They may also call themselves management consultants since they have done considerable work in business endeavors outside their coaching. Many problems faced by organizations are a combination of internal and external issues, which clouds the traits of who is a business coach and who is a business consultant.

NEW WORLD ORDER OF BUSINESS

In recent years the global world of business has seen many great changes that have impacted organizations and resulted in their need for consultants to help them deal with these new complexities. These include the rise of the Asian economies and rapidly changing technologies. Another has been continued changes in how businesses hire. Many companies want to minimize the number of full-time employees and seek more on-demand experts as needed. Currently, 30% of the US workforce is contingency workers, such as temporary, part-time, independent contractor, virtual, and on-call. Some estimates project 40% of the US workforce will be such workers by the 2020s. Employers can cut back on overhead by using consultants and on-demand workers rather than full-time employees and avoid healthcare, training, pension, etc., costs.

AVOID LAYOFFS

Consultants can be a much needed auxiliary workforce when permanence is not necessary. When you hire consultants you avoid layoffs. Layoffs can give the impression that a company is having financial problems when in reality some of their workers aren't necessary on a full-time basis. When the job is finished the consultant leaves, returning at a later date. You may even be able to keep using the same consultant and skip the learning curve. Small companies in particular can't afford the hiring of full-time specially skilled employees that are needed intermittently.

MAJOR TECHNOLOGICAL & SOCIETAL CHANGES

Advanced technologies such as robotics, artificial intelligence, internet of things and blockchain have made consultants who know what they are doing a critical need for many organizations. These are part of the Fourth Industrial Revolution that are combining physical, digital and biological technologies into a very disruptive force for the way we live and work. The large multinational business consultancies as well as some small consulting firms have varying degrees of expertise in successfully helping to integrate these new technologies.

It remains to be seen how many jobs will be gained and lost as these advanced technologies are incorporated. Will there be a small elite workforce that will be in charge of this new technology and vast numbers of workers who will no longer be needed? If this is the case, how will the redundant white-collar and blue-collar workers pay for the necessities of life? Many kinds of consultants continue to be hired by the private as well as the public sector to help resolve these kinds of issues.

DISRUPTION OF CONSULTING INDUSTRY

Consulting is undergoing many changes, just like the retailing, transportation and lodging industries. Many are questioning whether there is value in using consultants, whether there is a positive return on such an investment. There are no easy answers because of the many variables. For one, the consultants actually doing the work at the large, name-brand multinational consultancies may undergo a major disruption in part because the people on the ground doing the consulting only receive a fraction of the revenues generated by their work. The rest goes into overhead such as fancy skyscraper offices, furnishings and the bureaucracies that sustain these companies. The huge and truly complex projects might best be left to the huge consultancies, but a question to be asked is whether the approaches used by the big companies are the most valid means to find solutions or there may be simpler methodologies at a much lower cost provided competently by smaller firms.

HOW BUSINESS CONSULTANTS & COACHES CAN HELP YOUR ORGANIZATION

A number of examples have been given to demonstrate how businesses use the assistance of consultants and specialized consultative business services for a wide variety of needs. These samples give a broad perspective. There are many variations, nuances and complexities that enter into what they do that are beyond the intent of this book. Business coaches and consultants are also very active in government and nonprofit organizations to improve their performance.

CONSULTANTS MAY SAVE YOU A GREAT DEAL IN THE LONG RUN

Consultants could help a company, public entity, or non-profit organization save money in many ways. You are purchasing knowledge by hiring a consultant. A small investment in expertise relative to your entire budget could result in a great return on investment. For example, a negotiation consultant could work with a manufacturing company, hospital group, etc., to improve how they negotiate, thereby saving them thousands of dollars a year. Coaches who solve problems can also be of great value by improving organizations.

Geoffrey Michael (www.geoffreymichael.pro) in New Hampshire has saved companies nationwide a great deal of money through his negotiation consulting and training seminars. The costs of such consultant services are typically more than offset in the first negotiation, and the savings will continue to accrue for the long-term benefit of the company. This type of cost trade-off can be expected from consultants who improve operations in their selective areas of business expertise. In other words, experienced and knowledgeable consultants will more than pay for themselves, very often many times over.

Public Safety Specialists Group (www.pssg.net) of Illinois advises public safety agencies such as police and fire departments in the US and globally how to operate more efficiently, save money and plan for the future.

SOLVE PROBLEMS

Consultants can help diagnose and solve problems and generate alternative solutions to problems. Often they can identify hidden problems that businesses didn't know they had. The suggestions consultants make are just that, suggestions that do not have to be wholly implemented and can instead be only partly applied or just considered. It isn't unusual for millions of dollars to be spent on major consulting projects whose suggestions are never fully implemented.

TUNE UP AN ORGANIZATION

Some managers are too tightly intertwined with their company and may benefit from consultants' outside perspective to operate more efficiently. You might need someone to identify how to operate more efficiently and remove dead weight. It is easy to become entrenched with procedures that should be streamlined or with parts of the company that should be sold off.

Dimensional Growth in Illinois (www.dimensionalgrowth.com) has been successful with many performance improvement projects and developing high performance organizations.

BCA Consultores (baltarconsultores.com) advises its clients how to design and implement a new organizational structure, review, update and automate processes using appropriate technology. They assist in the preparation of a process manual, with a description of the functions and responsibilities of each position.

VALIDATE IDEAS

Senior management may have come up with some proposed changes but is unsure if these are going in the right direction. An expert review of these changes could validate or negate what management has proposed or result in enhancements of these changes.

ADVICE ON TECHNOLOGY, INVESTMENTS, MARKETING & OTHER SPECIALIZED NEEDS

Both small and large organizations require much expertise and specialized knowledge, such as digital technology, engineering, architectural design, marketing, healthcare, etc., at various times. Many consultants and specialized service providers are employed in this category. For example, Fortium Partners (www.fortiumpartners.com) is a substantive consultancy that provides technology advisory services to: align the company's business and technology strategies so the company can achieve its strategic goals; review and provide advice on critical business decisions (and risk) such as M&A, ERP evaluation and selection, critical project management or rescue. A number of other examples are given to show the diversity of what functions may be considered as business consulting.

SOLVING MARKETING, DISTRIBUTION & SALES PROBLEMS

GLOBALLY

TRC Chicago (www.thereillycompany.com) provides solutions to management, marketing, distribution and sales problems worldwide. This is done through corporate performance assessment, revenue generation, international expansion, channel management in international markets, structural recommendations & implementation and interim managers.

SOFTWARE CONSULTING

Capitol Strategies Consulting (www.capstratconsulting.com) and Profi Solutions (www.profisolutions.com) offer software solutions. Another software developer is James Bridgewater, Ph.D., who develops software for both scientific applications, such as computational neuroscience and enterprise e-commerce. He also has worked in the semiconductor business in writing software to help facilitate the design of integrated circuits (www.linktwentytwo.com).

Much software consulting is outsourced globally since it can easily be done remotely at lower costs and comparable quality in the less prosperous countries provided the service providers have the necessary skills. Rishabh Software & Engineering (rishabhsoft.com) is a major Indian outsourcer that assists international companies from a variety of industries.

Those needing assistance with the development of virtual reality, augmented or mixed reality, 3D models or interactive apps can turn to Prefixa (www.prefixa.com), a Silicon Valley and French creative high-tech virtual reality company that changes industries. Your developments can be useful to increasing the success of selling your products or projects and facilitating the decision-making process of your customers with interactive 3D and VR. They offer software development, engineering and industrial design, virtual reality applications and interactive applications. Their multidisciplinary experience allows them to focus not only on design and engineering, but also on the commercial and market needs that always seek business success.

For companies that currently sell software products or services in their market and want to sell their products in another country, Intechnational LLC (Intechnational.com) is a Silicon Valley-based consulting firm specializing in international business development. Their team has extensive international experience supporting technology companies to help them explore, validate, enter and expand business internationally.

CYBERSECURITY

Cybersecurity experts are a common expertise called upon by organizations of all sizes. Consultants can provide such intermittent assistance for days, months and even years depending on the needs of the client.

Intelisec in Illinois (www.intelisec.com) helps small to medium businesses keep data secure. Fortium partners provides C-level management consulting to help the company charter and implement policies and governances to achieve regulatory and industry compliance requirements.

4AC (4ac.com.mx), with offices in Mexico, Silicon Valley and Spain, is a company dedicated to providing security, infrastructure services and solutions in information technology to companies in highly regulated sectors. These include those in the financial sector that wish to solve, innovate or improve support with a team of engineers and specialized consultants.

They offer services such as consulting and implementation of SIEM solutions, vulnerability analysis, global network analysis among others. Their solutions utilize Juniper, IBM, Outpost24, Fortinet, Micro Focus and Solarwinds.

WELLNESS & FITNESS

A healthy workforce is more productive than one with many chronic problems. Leanness Lifestyle University (www.lluniversity.com) offers on-line corporate wellness/fitness programs used by corporations and government agencies.

ACCURATE TRANSLATION, TRANSCRIPTION AND INTERPRETATION

Artificial intelligence keeps getting better in language translation, but it still doesn't provide the accuracy of skilled human translators. Multilingual Connections (multilingualconnections.com) provides professional, accurate translation, transcription and interpretation services in over 75 languages to many corporate clients that require quality services.

CORPORATE GOVERNANCE CONSULTING

This is an example of a niche service that can be very useful for improving the performance of stagnant boards of directors. It is not uncommon that a corporate board of directors may be going through the motions of governance. Dana Saal at www.saalmeetings.com does this as well as working with associations as a management consultant.

TELEVISION PROGRAMMING CONSULTING

Scott Troeller's company Monticello Media (www.monticellomedia.net) has many years of experience in communications consulting for television networks and stations in how to improve their programming. He has produced and directed many television programs.

Hola Films (holafilms.tv), founded in 2012 by Carmen Aguirre, Daniel Guillen and Denisse Durón, is a production house in Mexico dedicated to producing videos. The combination of three different visions allows them to approach projects from different perspectives making each project a unique experience, with its own personality and voice.

INTERIM MANAGEMENT

Retirement, promotions, illness, maternity leave, sabbaticals, etc., could result in temporary vacancies in the management cadre that would be highly disruptive to the organization. Hiring a consultant could fill this gap and could go further to provide the benefit of having new skills to tackle challenging business issues. Also, a consultant who had skills to solve problems within that division, provide fresh ideas, or offer other needed assistance could be sought. If someone is hired to be a part of the company as a decision maker, that person would not be a 1099 employee but rather a W-2 employee who would be required to pay for taxes and social security.

Tom Murray is one of many Fortium Partners (www.fortiumpartners.com), a worldwide leader in providing technology leadership (CIOs, CTOs and CISO to companies of all sizes) through interim, fractional, virtual and permanent roles as well as advisory services for strategic initiatives with immediate engagement and simple terms. Fortium Partners helps clients achieve significantly better business outcomes than with traditional technology leadership roles.

They recommend that experts such as themselves be engaged before a merger, acquisition or critical technology decision to evaluate potential information technology difficulties that are inherent in the meshing of systems. Many of the Fortium Partners are former Fortune 500 company C-suite executives.

A TEST DRIVE

A variation of interim management is that if a long-term consultant has been effective and works well within the organization, this person might consider a full-time position. They could transition into full-time employment without a needing a learning curve; however, if this consultant works for a consulting firm, a finders fee would likely need to be negotiated.

VALIDATE & IMPROVE IDEAS THAT HAVE ALREADY BEEN GENERATED

An organization may have developed a new vision for its future, but be wary of certain aspects of these plans. A consultant can provide an outside perspective on these changes or give assistance with certain elements of their proposal.

ACCOUNTANTS MAY HELP IMPROVE YOUR BUSINESS

Experienced accountants have dealt with both successful and struggling businesses and have seen a lot through the years, resulting in being able to foster wisdom on the inner workings of businesses. Some accounting firms have skilled management consultants. While many don't have the skills or insight for complex projects, they could well be able to consult in matters like business efficiency and business turnaround. In a smaller community the only consulting assistance available is likely to be an accounting or legal firm.

ATTORNEYS ARE OFTEN KEY PLAYERS

Legal counsel is integral to many business functions. Not using business lawyers for advice could eventually result in bankruptcy if wrong decisions are made and the company loses a major lawsuit. Running something legally is a frequent precaution to make sure a decision will not have negative consequences. Smaller companies usually don't have lawyers on staff, while larger companies may have legal staffs that outside lawyers supplement for special needs.

The Madrid Crost law firm in Illinois and New York (www.madridcrost.com) handles complex immigration law problems for businesses and individuals. This is just one business law specialty that includes criminal law, bankruptcy, construction law, employment law, estate planning, real estate, taxes, zoning, wills, trusts and probate estates. A lawyer is the first expert some businesses will turn to for business advice. In a smaller community, lawyers and accountants may be the only business experts available.

Founded by Jaime Millán, Integra Legal (integra.legal) is a business consulting firm specializing in the areas of corporate, tax and property law with an international reach. They have more than 30 years of joint experience in business management in Mexico through the detection, attraction and development of investment opportunities in the public and / or private sector through its multidisciplinary specialists with the commitment to achieve the objectives set by its clients.

The Guevara Intellectual Property firm (www.guevarapi.com), located in the Northwest of Mexico, is highly experienced in the management and protection of intellectual property and patents. Founded by Alan Guevara and Luisa Loustanau in 2008, it has helped raise awareness among many business entities and reinforced the importance of protecting intellectual property.

PROJECT MANAGEMENT

When a major project is about to be implemented, but the company's leadership feel their staff doesn't have the specialized expertise required to successfully implement the project, certain types of consultants provide project management assistance.

EXECUTIVE BUSINESS COACHING

A huge number of executive/business coaches provide their services across the US. Many companies have internal consultants who offer these services. Whether an organization withers or flourishes depends largely on the leaders' effectiveness in connecting with people inside and outside the organization. Ellen Hite from Insider Coaching and Consulting in Illinois (www.insidercoaching.com) specializes in thought leadership. Using neuroscience principles, she assists clients in discovering their motivational drivers and strategies for growth and significance.

A trained executive/business coach can work individually with company leaders as well as groups to get people out of ruts and help them think through problems. A coach asks questions, creates awareness, helps a client think through their needs and works with them to set their goals. A coach is not a therapist.

A common problem is executives are so focused on the present that they need someone with the skills to help them prepare for the future. Employees throughout the organization could also benefit from coaching to become more positive and engaged. Industrial psychology is a related field focused on increasing the productivity of organizations and improving the physical and mental well being of their workers.

Zynity (zynity.com) is an on-line executive leadership platform that brings together people, processes and technology to help teams be more effective individually and collectively.

Business coaches also are prevalent globally in the more developed countries. Elisabeth Carrio in France (http://elisabeth-carrio.com) works with companies of all sizes to identify and solve their internal problems and help with change. Her background in strategy, psychology, finance and organizations help her to be very versatile in the types of problems she can resolve.

TRAINING STAFF

Rapidly evolving technology and new government regulations can call for a consultant to train employees or your trainers on how to implement these changes and operate new equipment, technology and systems. They also work with human resources to do other types of needed instruction.

Grupo Interecta (grupointerecta.com) is a Mexican consulting and training company whose mission is to provide solutions and results requested by clients. In addition they design human resource training and development programs. These are oriented towards compliance with the interests and needs of the organization.

MARKETING/PUBLIC

RELATIONS/COMMUNICATIONS/DESIGN/MEDIA

Small to large organizations depend on marketing, advertising, public relations, design and related media consultants to various degrees. Some do much of this work internally, while others may delegate these functions to one company or breakout up to several consultants to do this work. They create and implement marketing strategies, make recommendations on where to spend money, build brands, create advertising and public relations messages, provide design services, etc. Turnover in these types of consultants can be high.

Andrew Bartlett's full-service creative agency (www.ootboxmedia.com) provides brand development, social media marketing, virtual reality strategies and aerial drone services. Betsy Van Die (www.writeperspectives.com) in the Chicago area has done much work in media and communications strategies, change communication and public relations. Her background in the medical, healthcare and wellness fields is noteworthy.

For those needing international marketing and communications assistance, Yana Fleming (yanafleming.com) works globally, particularly in emerging markets, where French, English, Spanish or Portuguese are the daily business language. She is experienced across multiple sectors of the communications industry and leverages in-depth knowledge of trends to execute effective multilingual integrated communications campaigns.

Hamster Sniper Advertising Company (hamsterysniper.com), founded by Carlos Castelo, is a boutique company dedicated to the creation of communication, branding and corporate identity strategies. It performs the functions of media center, advertising agency and marketing department outsourcing for companies. Their specialty is the development of advertising projects, corporate identity, sales strategies.

MEDICAL CONSULTING

The field of medicine is a huge business and has become very specialized. The primary care physician often needs to refer patients to a specialist. Large clinics can have hundreds of specialists. Even a specialist may need to refer a patient to a sub-specialist. The growing use of telemedicine makes it easier for a doctor to work with a specialist located elsewhere, hundreds or thousands of miles away.

In the large healthcare sector many consultants are involved with the development and manufacture of medical devices and supplies, research and technology, distribution and management of supplies so that they are available at the time of patient care. Having information and advice on access to public and private markets in the US, Europe, Latin America and elsewhere is key to achieving recognition and commercial success of the products, making the operation more efficient and obtaining greater profitability.

doHealth S.C. (www.dohealth.com.mx) advises companies and institutions that develop, manufacture and market medical technology. Their expertise includes market access, marketing studies and value chain analysis, business strategy, technology transfer, healthcare economics and regulatory considerations.

POLITICAL CONSULTING

Advising aspiring politicians with their political ambitions is a huge industry. They are deeply involved with determining what media to use and finding assistance from private sector companies. Some work with any political party while others stay with one party.

PROVIDE FRESH, OBJECTIVE VIEWS, STRATEGIES & PLANS

When an organization has been in operation and provided products or services basically the same way for many years, its leadership may want fresh views and unbiased opinions. How should it prepare for the future, what should it be selling, what are possible alternative strategies and how should these strategies be implemented? A company could well be operating in its comfort zone and not be prepared for dynamic changes, while a consultant could see the threats and opportunities differently when observing from an outside "big picture" perspective.

What makes planning difficult is the many external factors impacting a company that is out of its control. Even internal factors are hard to anticipate. Some scenarios can be forecast, while others are totally unexpected. The plans and strategies formulated from research may or may not be useful. Many companies think strategic planning has value since it gives an understanding of the many positive and negative internal and external forces at plan that can leave a company blindsided if not recognized promptly.

ASSIST WITH A MERGER, ACQUISITION OR STARTUP

If you plan to merge with, acquire, or start up a new division or company, expert assistance could be very helpful in avoiding major mistakes in the process or even finding reasons to not follow through with such plans. Once a merger or acquisition has been made, there are major cultural and other factors in this transition that consultants can help navigate.

Headquartered in Connecticut, Woodbridge International (www.woodbridgegrp.com) is a leading national and international mergers & acquisitions firm with 19 offices in North America, Europe, Asia, Latin America and the Middle East. They provide clients with the local knowledge and global reach they demand. The US team is committed to providing sellers with a dynamic global marketplace of buyers in which to find the best possible value for their company. If you are thinking of selling a company with $5 million to over $100 million in annual revenues, they welcome you to take advantage of their Free Value Assessment.

REVIVE OR SHAKE UP AND ORGANIZATION

A failing organization may need a consultant to suggest strategies and major changes to save a failing organization or help it adapt to new market conditions. An independent view from a consultant experienced in this work could help turn around a business, reorganize it, make it operate more efficiently and increase profits. Business coaches could bring forth ideas that improve management's performance and human interactions within the organization.

Marcelo Isaak was born in Bolivia (marcelo.isaak21@gmail.com) and graduated from Brooklyn Polytechnic (now part of New York University) as a mechanical engineer. His experience is in International Business Development, Performance Improvement, Establishment and Development of Operations, Industrial Products, Licenses and Acquisitions.

His global experience has been in the US, Latin America, Asia, Europe, Oceania and Africa. He's fluent in Spanish, English and Portuguese.

TURN-KEY PROJECTS

For turnkey projects the same contractor designs and builds a project. This may be done because the client doesn't have the expertise or sufficient staff to handle the project from concept to completion. Construction projects may be done this way as well as implementing major information technology changes. Training and continued updates and refreshers can be added to this.

MANAGED SERVICES

For example, in managed services, instead of a company creating a traditional marketing and communications department, this can be done by a consulting team integrating their services into the company. This option could provide the flexibility, cost-effectiveness, mobility and cutting-edge solutions to better thrive in a competitive environment. It might give the company's public relations and marketing efforts a higher return on investment than creating its own public relations and marketing department. If the client is not satisfied they don't have to shut down or reorganize their PR/marketing department but can find another managed services provider.

Kraftcomm Consulting Group (www.kraftcomm.org) in Illinois, which provides managed services in marketing and communications, is experienced in assisting multinational companies. Managed services could drive public relations and marketing efforts with a higher return on investment than creating its own PR, marketing department.

Managed services are common in information technology, particularly for smaller and mid-sized companies unable to afford IT staffs or preferring to outsource these services. One IT Managed Services Provider is STL (www.poweredbystl.com) in the Midwest. It has a state-of-the-art data center housed in a FEMA-rated underground bunker and meets Tier 3 standards, offering solutions such as Private CLOUD, Hosted Email, Virtual Desktop and Microsoft 365 services.

STL's cybersecurity experts keep business-critical data safe with early detection and response in its Security Operations Center (SOC). The

SOC leverages a combination of network perimeter defense, endpoint security vulnerability detection, extensive log analytics and customizable reporting. As a Fortinet® Gold Partner, STL uses the FortiGuard Indicator of Compromise (IOC) automated breach of defense system. The IOC continuously monitors client networks for hidden vulnerabilities, persistent attacks and advanced threats. Their managed services provide coverage from stringent compliance and audit requirements of SOC2, Type-2 HITRUST CSF*, HIPAA, PCI DSS and SSAE-16 reporting.

SCAPEGOAT

A company undergoing major financial problems combined with a declining economy and loss of markets likely believes that the best means of survival is downsizing. The workforce and local community, however, view senior management as being alarmist. The company, in order to implement the downsizing while minimizing negative reactions, hires a consulting firm to evaluate this plan. Although the likelihood is high that downsizing is needed to save the company, the company thinks it is best to have independent study results to verify this plan.

DETERMINING IF OUTSOURCING IS VALID

Is outsourcing products and services to foreign locations or even other parts of the same country beneficial to the bottom line? When all factors, such as transportation costs, tariffs, workforce quality, negative publicity, increased administrative costs, loss of control, political instability, etc., are considered, it may not be worthwhile or only so marginally worthwhile that the risk is not justified. An experienced consultant's perspective on this can sway the decision makers to make the most rational decision. Many of the Fortium

Partners have deep technology outsourcing (and in-sourcing) experience.

REMOTE EXPERTS CAN BE LESS EXPENSIVE

The properly skilled person already settled in a faraway place could save on travel expenses, lessen wear and tear on staff, and be considerably less costly for the services provided. In fact, some projects can be done better by someone already at the location who has local knowledge than sending someone there. Universities in even some of the more isolated countries are graduating talented individuals with excellent skills. Especially with modern telecommunications, person-to-person meetings are not always necessary so you can find the best and lowest cost consultant for a job regardless of location. Fortium Partners provides fractional and virtual technology leadership.

FOREIGN NATIONALS CAN BE INTEGRAL TO PROJECT SUCCESS

Some governments require the involvement of local citizens for various type of projects by outsiders or make the process for bringing in foreigners to do such work very complex. On-site foreign nationals, with local connections, knowledge of the culture, language, regulations, and business practices, can be integral to the project's success. India has a rapidly developing economy that is attracting much foreign investment. While it has simplified its bureaucratic steps for establishing a business, local assistance is paramount. China and many African countries also make it difficult to do business there without the involvement of knowledgeable local business people.

I. P. Pasricha chartered accountants and consultants (www.capasricha.com) in New Delhi, Mumbai, Gurugram and Ludhiana, India helps foreign companies establish themselves there and help with ongoing financial matters. They work on audits, taxes, mergers & acquisitions and outsource many services.

Intechnational LLC (Intechnational.com) is a consulting firm based in Silicon Valley that helps technology companies with their international business development and projects. Their team has extensive international experience supporting technology companies to help them explore, validate, enter and expand their business internationally. In addition, they provide support in international projects such as the organization of international conferences or events.

It has multilingual and multicultural consultants specialized in helping technology companies conduct international business in the United States. In addition, the consultants have carried out international commercial projects in Latin America, Europe, Asia and Africa. The experience of the team is specialized in technology, mainly in information technology.

COMPLEX JOB COULD BE BROKEN UP INTO SEVERAL CONSULTING JOBS

If a business has a job that requires expertise in several areas and it is difficult to find a person with sufficient knowledge in these disparate skills, why not break up the job and hire expert consultants as needed, particularly if there are seasonal variations in demand for this expertise? Much of this depends on what level of continuity and depth of knowledge are needed. For example, many organizations have a jack of all trades marketing manager without a staff. While such a person might be an excellent generalist, he or she may not have enough experience in public relations, mobile apps, digital advertising, big data or other skills to best meet the needs of the organization.

BUYING & SELLING BUSINESSES

Buying and selling a business can be very complex, particularly for larger businesses. Business brokers are intermediaries usually paid on commission to facilitate either the buying or selling a business. Often this is done confidentially so staff and customers aren't aware of the sale. They give advice and insight but often are not CPAs and attorneys, who are also brought into the process as the sale progresses. A commercial realtor may need to be brought in when real estate is involved.

The Business Exchange in Illinois and Missouri (www.theBX.com) has years of experience helping buyers buy and sellers sell businesses of all sizes.

HOW DO YOU FIND THE RIGHT CONSULTANTS AND COACHES?

First, is a consultant really needed? Do you really have a problem or need that can't be met with internal resources? Do you perceive your project to be worth the return on investment? Is a tune up or fresh perspective needed to improve the business?

Bear in mind that what you get may be volumes on analysis and recommendations that may just sit on shelves. If you want a more hands on approach, this must be stated in the scope of services in the contract. It is crucial you make this clear in the beginning stages of discussing your needs with potential consultants.

CONSULTING & COACHING ASSISTANCE ON THE CHEAP

You don't need to spend a lot or anything to get basic assistance. There are no cost and low cost alternatives if you put in the time to look. Keep in mind that the quality of what you get can be very mixed. While they may not provide a sophisticated work product, they could provide ideas you could discuss with another consulting firm or fellow peers.

A SMART FRIEND

You may know successful people who would be flattered if you took them to lunch and presented them with your business problems or challenges. You might get some good preliminary advice, but this person probably would not have the time to delve into the issue and have time to help like a paid consultant. They might possibly help and do a good job if you offered to pay them if they had spare time available.

COLLEGE PROJECT

Some universities awarding business degrees require their last year students to do a capstone project which entails working in a team on a real world consulting project. You might be able to find a class that would do such a project for your own firm. They could develop good alternatives or nuggets of advice, and this team likely would be under the direction of a professor who might even have been a consultant at some time or is currently doing consulting on the side.

INTERNSHIPS

You could hire a university intern in a BBA, MBA, finance, accounting, or other relevant program to assist you. Some of these students already have several years of substantive work experience, maybe even for a consulting firm, and want to enhance their credentials. They seek an interesting intern experience with challenges that give them meaningful responsibilities. Author Lothar Soliwon had graduate student interns for almost thirty years, with some of them already having had substantive work experience. They were able to accomplish complex projects and were as knowledgeable as some full-time consultants contracted by the organization.

SCORE

SCORE is a nonprofit organization with chapters across the US geared to volunteers assisting, coaching and advising small businesses with a variety of challenges. They help establish, grow and sell businesses. SCORE offers individual mentoring and many business training workshops. Visit www.score.org for more information.

SMALL BUSINESS DEVELOPMENT CENTERS

Small business development centers (SBDCs), which are located nationwide, assist and advise established businesses and entrepreneurs wanting to launch a business. Hosted by universities and state economic development agencies, they are funded in part by the US Small Business Administration, which assists with financing needs.

The SBDC advisors provide a variety of free business consulting and low-cost training services, business plan writing assistance, manufacturing assistance, lending advice, exporting and importing support, procurement and contracting help and other services to small businesses.

HIRING A PAID CONSULTANT OR COACH

Consulting firms vary from huge global management consultancies like McKinsey & Company, Boston Consulting Group, Accenture, and Bain & Company to thousands of small brick and mortar firms and home-based consultants. The very large ones have high overhead, can be very expensive, and are looking for major team projects that bring in hundreds of thousands of dollars. They might even be embedded within an organization for a long time. If you don't have much money, then you will be seeking a small consultancy. Quality can be excellent or poor with the smaller firms, but the smaller firms may have people who at one time worked for one of the big outfits. Small firms may be more creative since they don't have to follow a corporate culture of similar people like at a big firm. Creative types may not be appreciated at a big consultancy just as they are not well received at many huge corporations because they don't match the selection criteria established by human resources departments.

Large cities have many business consulting firms of varied competency. Just do an on-line search of "business consultant" or "business coach" and the name of the city and see what comes up. The availability and variety of skill sets of business consultants can be minimal in the smaller cities, where you can usually find accounting firms with CPAs of some competency. Their focus is skewed to accounting and related services. While having worked with many businesses they may be able to give you a basic analysis of your deficiencies and where to improve, they wouldn't have the needed skills for projects outside their realm of expertise. Chambers of commerce can provide you with names of consultants who are members, but that does not mean they are capable or have the expertise you need. Ask people you know for their recommendations.

The variations in certification, education, and training for business coaches and consultants can be huge, from people who haven't graduated from high school to MBAs and Ph.D.s. One doesn't necessarily need a graduate degree to provide a specialized service. Life and work skills may be more useful in some cases than the knowledge held by a fresh Ivy League business school graduate with limited real world experience.

The nature of the consulting business is cyclical variations of workload. Sometimes they are swamped and other times they may be spending considerable time on business development to expand their client base. The consultancy you choose may not be available immediately.

When inquiring at a consulting firm, you may speak with a senior manager who will say they will be a part of the team, but recent college graduates with varied levels of knowledge and experience could actually be doing most of the work. Make sure you speak with who will be doing most of the work and see if you are comfortable with them.

Some consultancies use artificial intelligence to various degrees to match their expertise with the needs of the client. If going in this direction you still need to do your due diligence to make sure the consultant(s) selected for you by the AI are capable of competent performance.

Getting a feel for how well you would get along with a business coach is usually not difficult because coaches are often in small or one-person firms. Some coaches sell multiple visit packages at a discount and others charge by the session. Coaching is done remotely anywhere in the world by some firms. Monique Daigneault (monique@executiveinfluence.coach) provides executive coaching on-site and remotely, including internationally. She helps her clients root out the cause of their pain points and implements solutions that are measurable and sustainable.

In many cases, you might be able to have the consultants do a small project first to see if they are competent, if they are easy to work with and responsive throughout the process, and how you like their results. Then you can go on to bigger things or do some trial and error with other smaller projects. You could try similar projects with another firm until you find the right one. Along the same lines for coaching have an introductory session before you make any commitment.

Since the freelance workforce is huge, there are a number of internet-based companies that provide workers on demand nationally and globally. Some of these are geared more to designers and writers, while others focus on IT and business. These are often remote workers. Examples of such companies are Fiverr, Guru.com, Upwork and Toptal, which provide a broad range of services. At some of these companies information about their consultants' backgrounds is not readily available from a website or a roster. Most lack transparency, which makes it difficult to determine who they have available and the skills they offer without going through a bureaucracy.

It is suggested that whatever you do, before you make a hire, research the prospective consultancy or coach and communicate with them to get a grasp on their experience and competency. Many references lack credibility or contain exaggerations. Others may essentially be character references and not give an evaluation of a consultant's skills. Many referrals are done as a favor for someone who may be a great friend, member of the same club or a golfing or drinking companion. References from former clients carry more weight, but even these may be skewed to generalities rather than skills and competence.

Selecting consultants and coaches should be given considerable time and thought. Communicate with the consultant(s) or coach to get a gut feeling if they seem a good fit to meet your needs. Are they familiar with your industry? Do they have the right skills for the task, particularly knowing the latest technology if that is why you need a consultant? Do they have experience, education, credentials, certifications, etc., that gives you confidence? Are they comfortable with dealing with your size of firm? Do you want someone who communicates and gets along with people well or do you primarily want a great technocrat to just do the job properly? Do they seem truly interested and excited about the project or do you get the feeling they can do it but basically would be going through the motions? Do they have the time to do your project properly? Are they available to continue to monitor the progress of their recommendations and give advice if you feel you need their continued involvement? These are all questions you may want to be answered before you can confidently move forward with a consulting firm or coach.

CONSULTING FIRMS OFFERING ONE-STOP SHOPPING FOR EXPERTISE

The largest of the global consulting firms and some smaller ones may offer one-stop shopping for a number of services for various functions in a variety of business and industries. If the consultants represented as experts are truly experts in their fields, using a one-stop shop make finding the right consultants and forming teams easier than going from firm to firm. Skepticism should arise if any one consultant claims to have a wide variety of expertise in many fields. They may know a lot generally but lack in-depth knowledge about some fields for which they state they have expertise.

INVOLVEMENT WITH CONSULTANT

The consultants may go through an information gathering period to fully understand your company. They may want to talk to various employees as part of their analysis. Do you have a problem with them poking around and asking questions? They may not learn as much as they want because some employees may be afraid of losing their jobs by giving candid answers. Learning by walking around gives them at least a cursory feel for the company. Depending on what they're contracted to do, they could need occasional assistance from management to make sure what they are doing is on course.

CONTRACTS & COMPENSATION

A simple word of mouth agreement can work if you are doing something simple with someone you know and trust, but even then you have no guarantee that a disagreement will not arise because of an honest misunderstanding. You need a signed letter of agreement or a formal contract giving a scope of services, compensation, confidentiality, escape clause, time frame, etc. Since contracts can become very complex, particularly for large projects, you may want to seek the services of an attorney.

Compensation can be hourly, for the entire project, based on performance or other plans and paid at intervals during the project or at the end. A deposit may be paid before the project begins. Low price does not necessarily correlate with limited competency and neither high price with highly proficient.

ZG WORLDWIDE CONSULTANTS CONNECTS CLIENTS TO BROAD RANGE OF HUMAN CAPITAL

When seeking consultants, a company to consider is ZG Worldwide

(Zukunft Group Worldwide LLC), which provides 90 associates across the United States and globally. Since many companies want fewer full-time staff and more on-demand experts, ZG Worldwide provides many technology, business, marketing & communications and healthcare solutions.

Many of their services can be provided remotely. They also offer long-term interim managers, a number of whom might transition to full-time employment for the rich opportunity. For those who find travel a strain or want to save on travel expenses or time, our professionals with MBAs, CPAs, M.D.s, Ph.D.s, etc., accept special assignments in many US states and many countries on six continents.

Being a member of Global Chamber (globalchamber.org), the only organization of its kind in the world gives ZG Worldwide supplemental assistance to tap into when there are country-specific and special requirements it can't fulfill internally. Global Chamber has a very diverse membership that includes many kinds of consultants, from the world's largest economies to developing nations.

ZG Afrika is a ZG Worldwide subsidiary that offers a variety of consultants and services in Africa and the Middle East. Africa is considered by many to be the "Continent of Future" as an investment frontier. Several countries are making much progress in overcoming some of their social and economic problems. Some countries are much better prospects for investments than others. ZG Africa's consultants are available to help businesses in many ways, particularly in dealing with country-specific bureaucratic problems where locals are better equipped to deal with complex red tape.

Visit www.zgworldwide.com or contact them at info@zgworldwide.com. They would be glad to send you their Roster of Associates that gives an expertise summary for each of their consultants in the US and globally.

ZG India is a partnership of ZG Worldwide and I. P. Pasricha (chartered accountants, tax experts, auditors, mergers & acquisitions experts, management consultants, etc.). With offices in New Delhi, Mumbai, Gurugram and Ludhiana, India they assist foreign companies in establishing businesses and other needs in the huge and fast-growing Indian economy. Indian firms gain access to many experts in the US. Visit www.capasricha.com for more information.

ABOUT THE AUTHOR

Lothar E. Soliwon   ZG Worldwide Consultants

Lothar is the President and CEO of ZG Worldwide Consultants, headquartered in Springfield, Illinois, USA, in the Central Illinois Technology Triangle. ZG Worldwide, a service mark of Zukunft Group Worldwide LLC, offers associates in 15 states and 25 countries. It provides services in business consulting, IT leadership, mergers & acquisitions, healthcare, marketing & communications, software and technology.

Originally from Germany, he was formerly a marketing manager, planner, consultant and administrator with the Illinois Department of Transportation in Chicago and Springfield, where he worked with the rail passenger, aviation and public transportation programs. Before that, he was an encyclopedia writer in Chicago. Lothar has a liberal arts undergraduate background in geography and holds an MBA and Master of Social Sciences from the University of Illinois. He describes himself as a business generalist. Outside of work he has long been interested in fitness, reading, economics and history.

ABOUT THE COEDITORS

Coeditor Christian Aguirre is a business consultant and entrepreneur in Hermosillo, Sonora, Mexico. Coeditor Donaji Montes is President of Intecnational, a Silicon Valley business and technology consulting company in San Jose, California, USA that operates internationally.

CONNECT with the TECHNOLOGY SPECIALISTS You NEED

MANAGED IT SERVICES
Small- to medium-sized businesses can enjoy the benefits of a professional and scalable expert IT staff to meet specific operational needs without hiring multiple vendors or creating an internal IT department.

CYBERSECURITY
Our cybersecurity emphasis is on early detection and response rather than building barricades that no longer stop hackers. We combine a strong security posture with a formal incident response plan. Hence, this greatly reduces the odds and average cost of a data breach.

TECHNOLOGY LEADERSHIP
We provide short- to long-term CIOs, CTOs, and CISOs, former Fortunue 500 C-suite executives who will come to Central Illinois.

ADVANCED HAND-HELD ULTRASOUND DEVICES
- Revolutionary wireless ultrasound systems from Sonostar start at just $1,499.
- Transmits quality image via built-in Wifi hotspot to any type of screen.
- Multiple medical uses.

TECHNOLOGY CONSULTING
- Expert-level Analysis
- Design
- Development
- Project Management
- Futurist
- Business Analytics
- Solution Architectural Design

SOFTWARE DEVELOPMENT
- Business Software
- Government Software
- Scientific Software
- Mobile Apps
- E-commerce Websites
- CRM Development

In today's business environment, companies want **less** full-time staff and **more** on-demand experts.

ZG Worldwide provides a **single source** for solutions in:
- Technology
- Business
- Marketing
- Communications
- Healthcare

To get a **FREE** assessment, and to connect with our expertise, contact us today at

info@zgworldwide.com
or
217-691-0554

zgworldwide.com — ZG WORLDWIDE CONSULTANTS

ZG Worldwide Consultants is the service mark of Zukunft Group Worldwide LLC.

www.ingramcontent.com/pod-product-compliance
Lightning Source LLC
Chambersburg PA
CBHW072301170526
45158CB00003BA/1142